QUILTING

QUILTING

Jennifer Rollins

CRESCENT BOOKS
NEW YORK • AVENEL, NEW JERSEY

Previous page: Small red satin bows visually hold this cheerful quilt together.

This 1994 edition published by Crescent Books,
distributed by Outlet Book Company, Inc., a Random House Company,
40 Engelhard Avenue, Avenel, New Jersey 07001

Random House
New York • Toronto • London • Sydney • Aukland

First published in 1992
Reprinted in 1993
Reprinted in 1994

Publishing Manager: Robin Burgess
Project Coordinator: Lynn Bryan
Project assistant: Jenny Johnson
Editor: Dulcie Andrews
Illustrator: Carol Ohlbach
Photographer: Andrew Elton
Designer: Kathie Baxter Smith
Typeset in the U.K. by Seller's
Produced in Singapore by Imago

Title: Country Crafts Series: Quilting
ISBN: 0 517 08799 5

CONTENTS

INTRODUCTION

The popularity of creating a beautiful piece of craft by hand is increasing among people of all age groups.

Through this Country Craft series, it is our hope that you will find satisfaction and enjoyment in learning a new skill, in this case quilting.

More and more people are turning to the old-fashioned skills which enabled our grandmothers to make their homes colorful and comfortable. Once you have mastered the basic steps, creating your own quilt designs will bring you much pleasure, as you will discover.

Opposite: This beautiful white-on-white cot cover is a fine example of Trapunto quilting.
Design by Narelle Grieve.

HISTORY OF QUILTING

PATCHWORK AND QUILTING dates back more than 2,000 years. However, it was not until the 18th century that the designs with which we are familiar today were developed. Often a quilting pattern had its basis in other needlework such as embroidery but, as time passed, designs such as feathers, cables, flowers, leaves and diamonds became part of the quilter's repertoire.

In England before the 1700s, quilting was used mainly on solid color quilts or to outline crewelwork (embroidery) on bedcovers. An early and very simple type of patchwork was the 'strippy' quilt, where long strips of plain fabric were joined together and then quilted with elaborate motifs. In the 18th and 19th centuries, patchwork and appliqué also became popular and it was the latter style particularly that gave rise to new creativity in quilting design. With the advent of faster, cheaper fabric production and a greater choice of colors, quilters were able to create more varied and colorful designs and these in turn, provided the impetus for a more imaginative use of the quilting stitch.

When the first English and Dutch colonists arrived in North America, times were hard. Fabric, even for utility items such as bedding, was scarce. From this austerity grew a creed of thrift and an abhorrence of waste which encouraged women to use every last scrap of fabric in their quilts. Their legacy today is the scrap quilt, a vibrant combination of shirt and dress fabrics that joined every conceivable stripe, spot, floral and geometric pattern into designs which are as fresh now as they were when they were created.

In the mid-19th century the price off a fabric dropped as production techniques improved. North America was then producing its own fabric instead of importing it from England. New and more permanent colors began to become available. Even feed sacks were printed with attractive floral designs and thrifty farming women added these to their quilting scrap bag.

Around this time, signature quilts began to make their appearance. They were composed of signed blocks in quilting or ink, sometimes accompanied by appliqué or patchwork. These were usually designed as presentation quilts for a couple about to be married, for a valued member of the community, or for other special occasions such as births or baptisms.

The most intricate and finest quilting was usually reserved for appliquéd quilts which were kept for 'best' or not displayed at all, so these quilts are the ones that are best preserved today. Many more of these have survived

Opposite: The richness of color in the quilted piece and the combination of fabric in the patchwork cushion are important design elements.

than the utility quilts which, having done their service, often became the filling for other quilts. Utility quilts were usually coarsely quilted with a simple pattern, either following the line of the patchwork, or in an overall design such as a grid or radiating half circles, also known as the 'Baptist Fan' quilting, which could be easily marked on the quilt with a compass and pencil.

After the decline in popularity at the end of the Victorian era of the 'crazy quilt', which used silks, velvets, lace and wool in combination with embroidery instead of quilting, general interest in quilting and patchwork diminished. In the 1920s a revival occurred and this interest continued, fed by a wide range of inexpensive fabrics and the growth of magazines and mail order catalogs devoted to quilters' needs, until WWII.

During the war, women had less time and money to spend on such activities as quilting. Fabric became expensive and scarce. When the war was over, the modern age had arrived and with it, the advent of manmade fabrics, 'space age' furniture and prefabricated houses. Quilting was considered a thing of the past.

A second revival has occurred over the past 20 years, fueled not only by an interest in antiques of the North American colonial period but also, in this age of high technology, by a need of many people to return to the more measured pace that the technique and creativity of quilting requires.

Quilting is not restricted to warm and weighty bedcovers. It can be adapted for cushion covers, cot and crib quilts, and wall hangings. A hand-quilted bedcover makes a

A typical example of the 'Baptist Fan'
patchwork design.

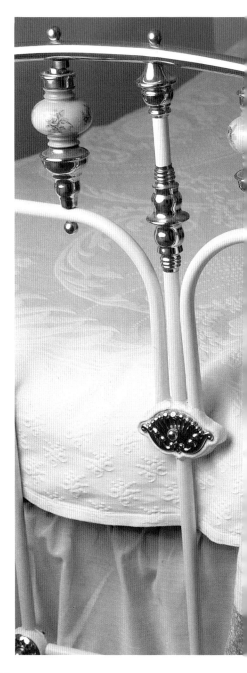

unique wedding present or gift for a new grandchild and, if it is well looked after, it will be prized for generations.

This book will give you all the basic information for designing, making and caring for a handmade quilted piece. It will probably create an interest too, that will have you scouring quilting stores and bookstores for more patterns, fabric and ideas. The good thing about a quilting addiction is that it involves so many different aspects of needlework, such as design, color coordination, cutting and quilting, that it is creative and relaxing at the same time. Who could ask for more, either as a hobby or a full-time occupation?

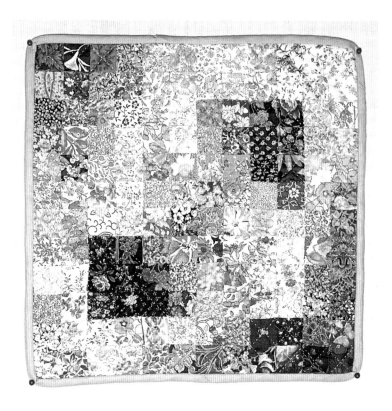

A miniature quilt designed by Billie Jacobsen.

TOOLS AND MATERIALS

FOR QUILTING you need very few tools and materials other than what you already have in your sewing basket.

Needles The basic rule to remember is 'the shorter the needle, the smaller the stitch' Size 7 to 8 'betweens' are ideal although you may need some practise in using such a short needle when you first begin.

Thimble A well-fitting thimble with a flat tip is essential for pushing the needle through the three layers of fabric in a quilt. The thimble should not be too tight or too loose and it is worth experimenting with a few different styles to find the one that suits you.

Fabric markers You will need some kind of pencil or pen to mark your quilting design onto the fabric. Many quilters use an HB pencil to mark the design, however, I have found an impermanent fabric marker is effective. You can draw the design quite heavily on the fabric and the mark is easily removed with a damp cloth. (Always test a small piece of fabric with the pen before marking the quilt top.)

Quilting thread Always use quilting thread instead of ordinary thread when quilting. It is slightly thicker, it is a lot stronger and it is less likely to knot or tangle. Quilting thread is available in a wide variety of colors to match your fabrics.

Beeswax Many quilters use a block of bees wax through which they run the thread before quilting. The beeswax helps prevent tangles and it smooths the progress of the thread through the fabric.

Batting Batting is the material that forms the middle layer of the quilt and the choice of batting will largely determine the final appearance of the quilt. There are many types of batting available, from the polyester batting found in most fabric stores, to wool, cotton and high, medium and low loft battings available from quilting stores.

For the beginner the medium or low loft polyester batting is probably the simplest to work with. The needle slips through the batting easily and the quilt top does not need to be densely quilted to hold the batting in place. For a puffier quilt, high loft batting is the choice, whereas for a more traditional, flat appearance, cotton, wool or low loft batting is suitable. Remember that cotton and wool batting must be densely quilted. If large areas are left unquilted, the batting may bunch and become unevenly distributed.

Quilting frames To achieve a smooth, even appearance to the quilt, the top, middle, and backing layers must be stretched while they are being quilted together. If the project you are working on is a small one, for example, a cushion cover or cot quilt, a quilting hoop or a small frame will hold sections of the work taut while you quilt. As one section of the quilt is finished, the hoop or frame is moved to the next section to be quilted.

masking tape

batting (wadding)

quilting thread

template plastic

ruler

dressmaking scissors

embroidery scissors

needles

thimble

beeswax

rubber

fine marker pen

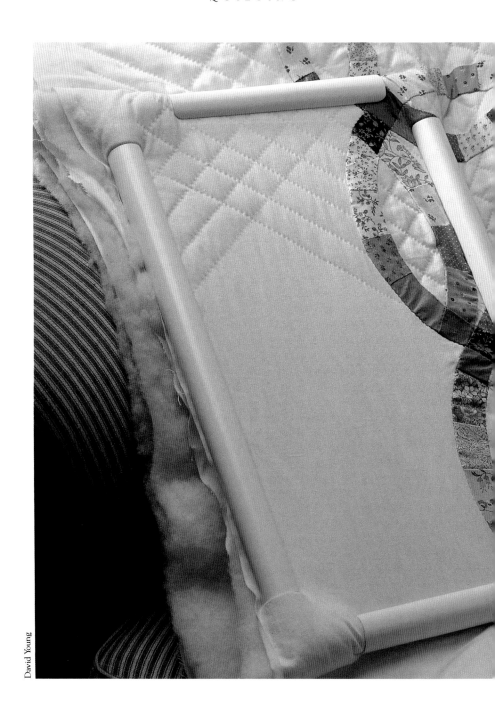

David Young

For larger projects, such as a bed-sized quilt, a full-sized frame that will hold the entire quilt is ideal, although it is not necessary. It is possible to buy these large frames ready-made, but do-it-yourself frame patterns are available at a much lower cost.

Template plastic   This is a piece of stiff plastic that is cut into a quilting design, for example, a chain pattern, a leaf or a flower design and is used to mark a design onto the quilt top. Plain template plastic and ready-cut templates in a wide range of designs and sizes can be bought from specialty quilting stores.

Masking tape   This is used when you want to quilt large areas in straight lines, such as in some of the filling patterns. It can be re used a number of times.

Other   There are a number of other items which are useful when designing and making a quilt. These include a ruler (marked in both centimetres and inches), a sharp pair of scissors to cut threads, an eraser (for rubbing out pencil marks on your quilt), a steam iron, a deflated balloon or large rubber band (for pulling the needle through the fabric layers), and pieces of card for making into templates.

*The edge of a quilt in a frame ready
for stitching.*

QUILT DESIGN

THE QUILTING STITCH can be used in a number of ways depending on the type of quilt you are going to make. If you have already pieced a patchwork top, the quilting stitch you use can either outline the design already created with the colored fabric shapes, or it can contrast with the design. It depends on the effect you want to create.

Outlining the pattern created by the patchwork blocks may be done by simply following the design with a single row of quilting stitches, either 'in the ditch', that is, in the seam between two patchwork pieces,

or 1/8 inch outside the design (Fig. 1).

Selectively outlining certain parts of the patchwork block can create a secondary design which will add interest to the complete quilt (Fig. 2). Contrast quilting where, for example, a curvilinear quilting design over a geometric fabric pattern is used, can also look effective.

'White-on-white' quilts use only the quilting stitch on a plain background to create the pattern; as the name suggests, there is no patchwork piecing involved.

'White-on-white' quilts require more planning at the design stage. A quilt of this

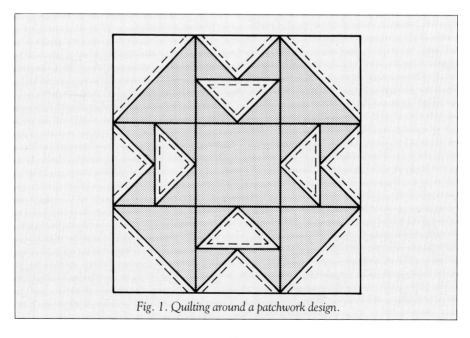

Fig. 1. Quilting around a patchwork design.

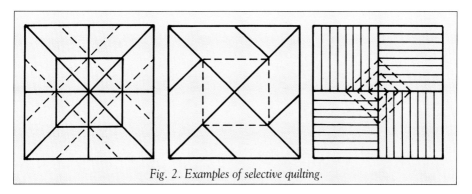

Fig. 2. Examples of selective quilting.

kind usually consists of five design elements.

The first and most important element is the central motif, made up of one or more elements that are repeated and reversed to form a circular, oval, square, or diamond-shaped design.

The secondary design, placed between the borders and center of the quilt, repeats or emphasizes certain elements of the central motif. In between the central and secondary motifs is the filling design, and the borders and corners make up the fourth and fifth

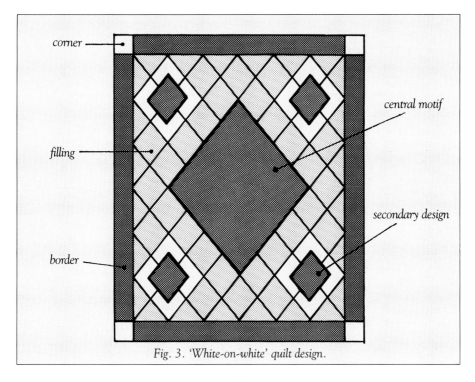

Fig. 3. 'White-on-white' quilt design.

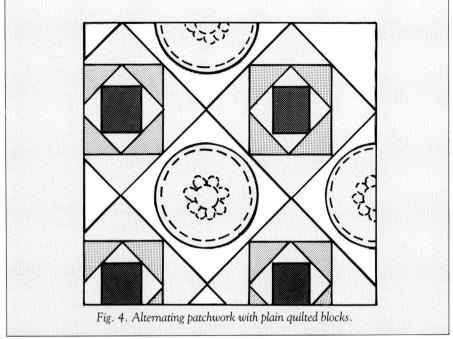

Fig. 4. Alternating patchwork with plain quilted blocks.

parts of the design (Fig. 3).

However, a much simpler quilt can be designed, using only the central motif, filling design and border elements. It depends on how ambitious you are and how much time you have at your disposal.

A combination of the above styles can be used alternating colored blocks of patchwork with plain blocks (Fig. 4). In this case, the quilted plain blocks should not dominate the entire quilt, but should emphasize certain aspects of the patchwork blocks, such as pinwheels, geometric elements or flowers. You can be quite creative with single quilting motifs, making them as detailed or as simple as you want.

A contrast effect can be obtained by, for instance, creating a circular design in the plain blocks, alternating with a geometric pattern in the patchwork blocks. Try to keep one element of the design consistent across all blocks to tie the quilt together.

Opposite: This 'Wedding Ring Tile' pattern provides large plain blocks for quilting.

TECHNIQUES OF THE CRAFT

HAVING DECIDED on a quilting design, you are now ready to assemble the quilt 'sandwich'. This sandwich consists of the backing fabric, the quilt batting, and the quilt top.

When planning the size of the quilt, remember to add extra to the length and width of the bed. See the chart for details.

MATTRESS	SIZE
Standard cot	51 x 27 1/2 inches
Standard single bed	75 x 39 inches
Standard double bed	75 x 53 inches

As a general rule, to calculate the quilt size for a single bed, add 8 inches to the length of the mattress for the pillow tuck. Also add 18 inches for the drop, 2 inches for shrinkage. Total: 103 inches for length.

For width, add 18 inch drop x 2 (for each side) and 2 inches for shrinkage. Total: 77 inches.

First of all, iron the backing fabric and the quilt top, taking care to iron all seam allowances to one side, rather than to either side, of the seam . Also insure that, if you have used patchwork in your quilt top, the darker seam allowances are ironed under the darker fabrics so they will not show through the lighter fabrics.

This is the last time you will ever iron your quilt, so it is important that all the wrinkles are removed at this stage.

Select an area large enough for you to lay out your quilt. If you have made a bed-sized quilt, the floor is probably the best choice, particularly if you can remove any rugs to prevent pins from sticking into the floor covering. Otherwise a large dining table or any large flat surface will do.

Lay out the backing fabric, wrong side up and lay the batting over it, making sure there are no lumps, thin spots or holes in the batting. Next, lay your quilt top over the batting, insuring that it fits squarely over the batting and backing fabric. Both the batting and backing fabric should be at least 2 inches larger than the quilt top.

Working from the center, secure all three layers of the quilt sandwich with large safety pins or tailor's pins. Use as many pins as you need to keep the layers from shifting or bunching. The quilt is now ready to be basted together.

Take a long piece of light-colored quilting thread (dark thread may mark light-colored fabric). Tie a knot in one end and, working from the center, make long basting stitches toward the edges of the quilt.

The quilt should be basted horizontally, vertically and diagonally and care should be taken to insure that all three layers are caught up in the basting stitch (Fig. 5). If you are using a quilting hoop or small frame, additional basting is recommended (Fig. 6). Take

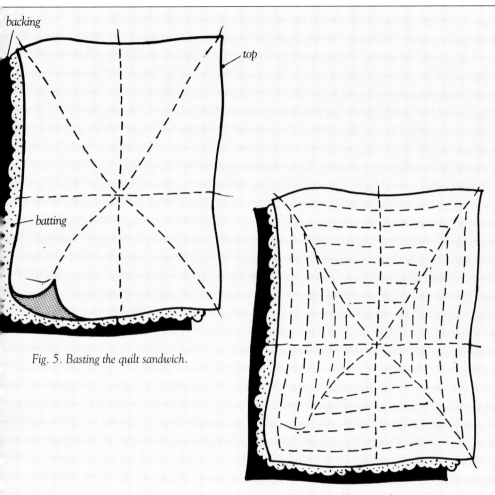

Fig. 5. Basting the quilt sandwich.

Fig. 6. Additional basting when using a
quilting hoop.

time and care with your basting and the finished quilt will have a professional, even appearance.

You are now ready to begin quilting. Place the quilt into the frame or hoop and insure that all three layers of the sandwich are held taut. (Some quilters say you should be able to bounce a coin on the surface of a quilt held in a quilting frame.)

When quilting you will need to wear a thimble on the third finger of your sewing hand in order to push the needle through the three thicknesses of fabric. Many quilters also use a thimble on the index or third finger of their other hand to help guide the needle back up through the layers.

Take a single length of quilting thread, thread the needle and make a knot at one end. Insert the needle through the fabric top and batting only, about 1 inch from where you want to begin quilting, guide the needle to the beginning of the quilting line, give a little tug, and the knot will disappear into the batting (Fig. 7).

A quilting stitch is a small running stitch. Push the needle at a slight angle until it pierces all three layers of fabric and comes in contact with your finger or thimble under-

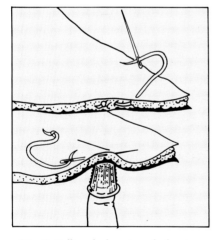

Fig. 7. Pulling the knot into the batting.

neath the quilt. Using this finger or thimble, guide the needle back up to the surface of the quilt and push the needle through. It is preferable to gather a number of stitches onto your needle before pulling the needle and thread. This helps establish a quilting rhythm which is very important in creating small,

even stitches and also insures that the stitches will be even on both sides of the quilt (Fig. 8).

The quilters' rule of thumb is eight stitches per 1 inch and the stitches should be the same size as the spaces between them. If you cannot achieve this goal at first, do not worry as your

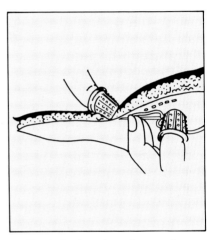

Fig. 8. Making the quilting stitch.

quilt will still look attractive even if the stitches are larger than eight to the inch.

Quilting through seam allowances makes it difficult to push the needle through and it will be necessary to make 'stab' stitches across the seam lines. Point the needle straight down and pull the thread through to the other side. Then repeat the operation in reverse, pointing the needle straight up toward the quilt top. Give an extra tug to the thread when working stab stitches.

To finish a quilting line, make a back stitch through the backing and batting only. Insert the needle through the same hole as you made this last stitch and draw it through the batting for about 1 inch. Pull the needle and thread taut and cut the thread close to the

Above: A collection of colorful quilts feature country images.
Following page: The pink quilt features a series of designs; the blue quilt has one central design.

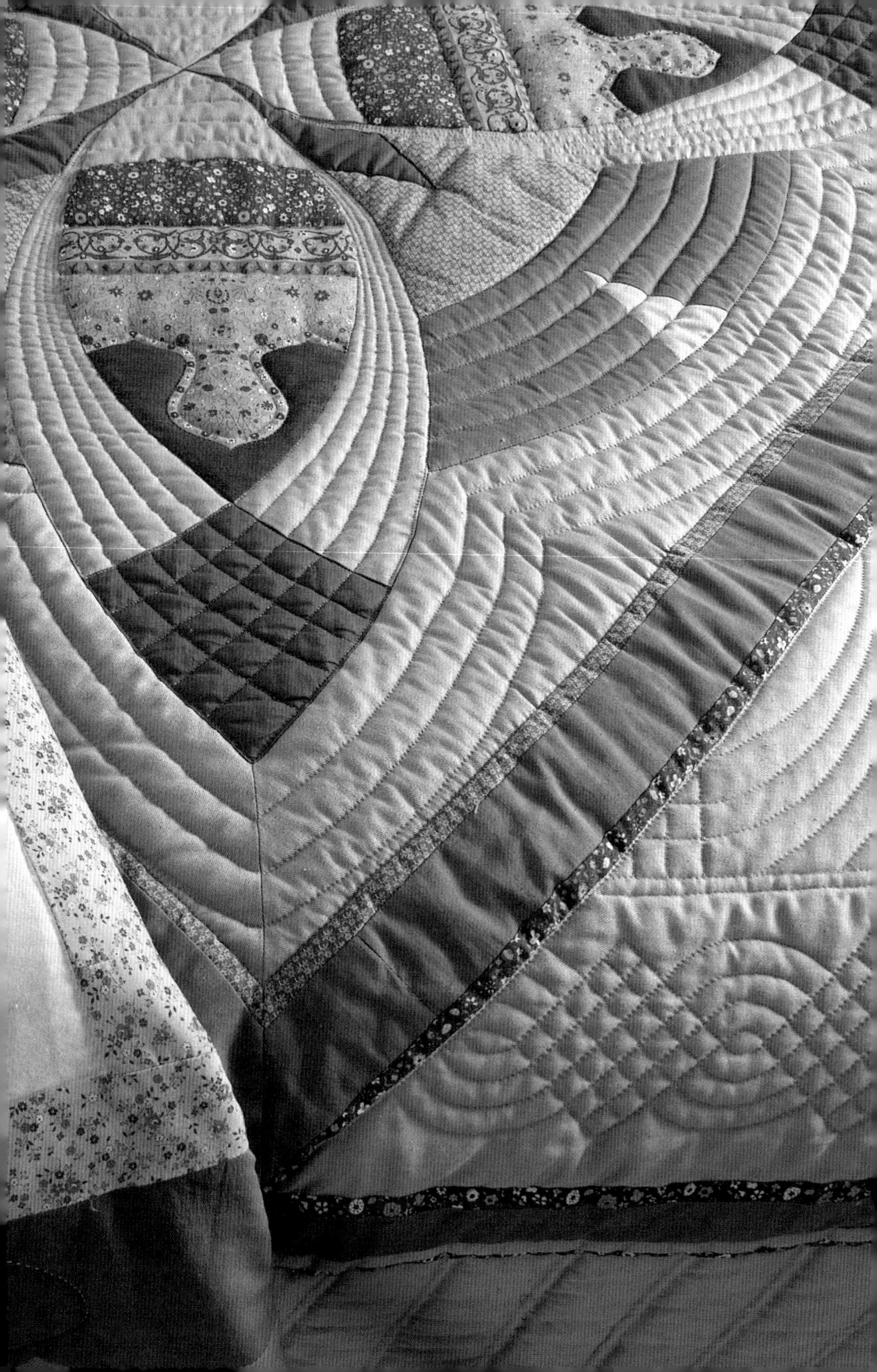

surface of the backing. The tail of thread will disappear into the batting (Fig 9).

Machine quilting is a method to consider if you need to finish off a quilt in a hurry, or if you like the effect of quilting, but do not enjoy the process.

Pin and baste the three layers as described

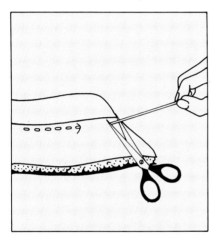

Fig. 9. Finishing a line of quilting.

for hand-quilting. Take one end of the quilt and roll it up tightly like a jelly roll until you nearly reach the middle of the quilt. Repeat the process at the other end of the quilt. There should be a space about 4-5 inches wide (Fig. 10). You will begin machine quilting in this area.

Some quilters use the ordinary sewing foot of their machines; however, most advise using either the quilting foot or the darning foot. The darning foot is especially useful because you can quilt forward, in reverse and in a circular motion. It takes quite a lot of practise to use a darning foot, once you have developed some expertise, it can make machine-quilting much faster.

Because there is no quilting frame to create tension across all three layers of the quilt sandwich, the quilt must be taken off the machine and tightly re-rolled after every few rows of quilting.

Use ordinary polyester or cotton thread

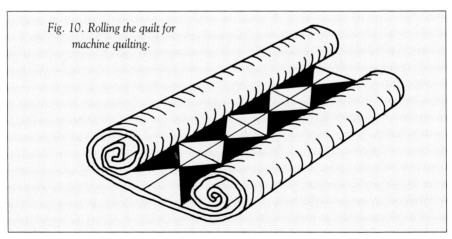

Fig. 10. Rolling the quilt for machine quilting.

Opposite: The design on this lovely teacosy was based on an early American block and adapted for this piece. Design by the Quilting Bee.

when machine-quilting. Some quilters use a combination of monofilament 'invisible' thread for the machine needle and ordinary thread in the bobbin. This will give a much softer appearance to the quilting than using cotton for both the needle and bobbin, which results in a solid quilting line. It is, however, entirely a matter of personal preference.

Tying a quilt is another effective way of finishing it off, especially if you have used a very puffy, high loft batting. In this case, tying is the method of choice because it is very difficult to hand-quilt an extremely thick batting.

The quilt sandwich should be prepared and basted in the same way as for hand-quilting. Mark with pins or a marker pen where you want the ties to be. If no hand-or machine-quilting is used in addition to tying, insure that the ties are evenly distributed across the

quilt to prevent bunching or shifting of the batting.

Note: Tying alone should not be used for wool or cotton batting which needs to be closely quilted.

Thread a sharp needle with some decorative yarn (good choices include thin ribbon, or wool) and push the needle directly through all three layers of the quilt. Leave about 3 inches of yarn above the quilt top (more if you will be tying bows). Bring the needle back up through the quilt, making a stitch about 1/8 inch long. Leaving the needle threaded, tie a square knot. Clip the thread and tie a double bow (Fig. 11). You may like to add a decorative bead or button to the bow.

If you do not want to make a feature of the ties, choose a yarn that will blend in with the quilt top and tie the knots on the back of the quilt instead.

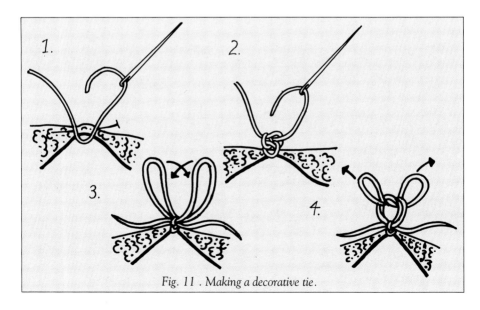

Fig. 11 . Making a decorative tie.

Above: Quilts are a charming addition to a bedroom. Many people treasure a favorite quilt for all their lives; the quilt becomes a family heirloom, handed down from generation to generation. Following page: This 'Wedding Ring' quilt has been quilted with a simple grid design.

Ian Tudor

FINISHING TECHNIQUE

THE FINAL STEP towards finishing your quilting project involves binding the edges of the quilt. The binding fabric may match the color of the outermost border or it may contrast with it, while matching one of the colors used in the quilt top. It should be the same fabric as the rest of the quilt and may be either straight grain or on the bias.

The width of the completed binding is usually about 3/8 inch. When cutting strips for the binding you will need to add 1/4 inch for each of the two seam allowances and another 1/8 inch to allow for the puffiness of the batting inside. Therefore cut a binding strip of approximately 1 inch in width.

Make sure that the basting or quilting stitches hold all three layers of the quilt sandwich together. Trim the backing and batting 3/8 inch from the seam line, which will insure that there is enough batting to fill the binding when finished.

Pin the binding strip to the topside of the quilt sandwich with right sides together. There should be about 2 inches of extra binding on either end of the border. Sew through all four layers, binding, quilt top, batting, and backing fabric with a 1/4 inch seam. It is best to use a sewing machine for these as the seams will be much stronger and more even. Complete the two opposite bindings first, then fold the corner edges of the bindings out of the way and sew in the other two bindings, finishing

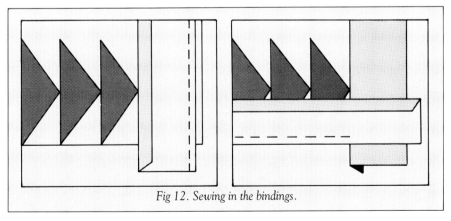

Fig 12. Sewing in the bindings.

Opposite: A sampler quilt by Dianne Finnegan is a series of traditional patterns and incorporates many visual ideas gained from her travels. A block at the top right-hand corner was inspired by tessellated floor tiles she saw at Rochester Cathedral.

just inside the already sewn binding, about 1/4 inch from each edge (Fig. 12).

Turn the quilt to the back and pin the binding, turning under the 1/4 inch seam allowance as you go. Whipping stitch or blindstitch into place.

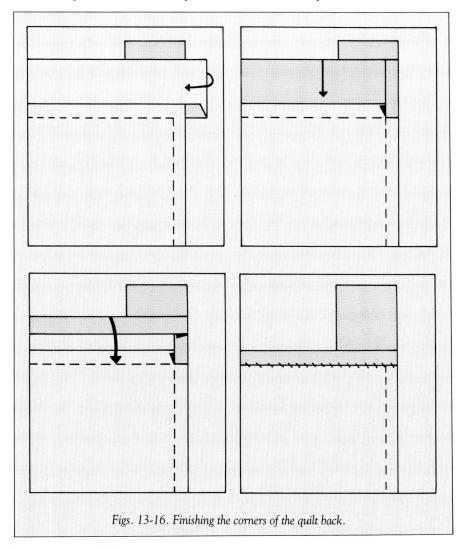

Figs. 13-16. Finishing the corners of the quilt back.

Opposite: Ann Haddad's 'Little Homestead Quilt' features six different house designs in various fabric patterns. The plain blocks are traditional Sashiko patterns. The work is machine-pieced and hand-quilted.

Rob Tawton

At each end, trim the binding to 1/4 inch, tuck in the edges and whipping stitch a squared corner (Figs 13-16).

Fold the other bindings to the back of the quilt and pin and stitch in place. When you reach a corner edge, push the needle through to the front where the two bindings meet.

On the front, trim the loose binding to 1/4inch extra and fold it on the diagonal to form a mitered edge. Blindstitch in place (Fig. 17). Turn the quilt to the back, tuck in

around the corners.

Your quilt is now complete and after the many hours of labor you have spent on it, you will want to care for it properly.

Avoid placing your quilt on a bed or wall in direct sunlight – the sun will fade the colors and weaken the fibers.

If your quilt is used as a bedcover, fold it down toward the end of the bed before you go to sleep or, if the quilt is for added warmth, fold the top part of your sheet over the quilt.

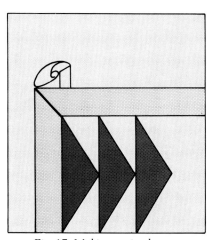

Fig. 17. Making a mitred corner.

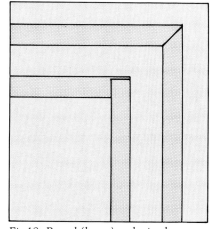

Fig 18. Butted (lower) and mitred corners.

the ends and blindstitch the fold, either making a butted edge or another mitered one (Fig. 18).

If you are using continuous bias binding, start at the center of one side of the quilt . Pin or baste the binding in place, making one or two folds in the binding to ease it around the corners. Machine-sew the binding, blind-stitch the join where the two ends of the binding meet, roll the binding over to the back of the quilt and blindstitch or whipping stitch the binding in place, again easing it

This avoids excessive soiling, which is worth-while since washing quilts can be difficult.

When washing a bed-sized quilt choose a container that can take the quilt without squashing it. A tub is ideal. Dissolve some washing powder in plenty of warm, not hot, water and add the quilt, gently squeezing and moving it around in the water. Rinse thoroughly and wring it as dry as possible without tugging and pulling – this could weaken the seams.

The weight of a wet quilt also puts a strain

on the seams so it is best to lay it out flat on the ground, protecting the underside with a sheet. Dry the quilt away from direct sunlight.

Quilts can also be machine-washed, but there is no advantage to this unless the drum of your machine is large enough to allow the quilt free movement through the water. Do not cram a large quilt into a small washing machine; the quilt will not be cleaned properly and both the quilt and the machine could be damaged.

If you have a good-sized washing machine, use a gentle cycle with warm water and run the spin cycle only long enough to get out the bulk of the water.

If you do not have enough space to lay the quilt out flat, use the washing line, but hang the quilt over two or three parallel lines, instead of just one. Again, this lessens the strain on the seams and the quilt will dry more quickly too.

Store an unused quilt in a cloth bag or pillowcase with layers of acid-free tissue paper between the folds. Never use plastic, as air needs to circulate around the quilt. Do not store a quilt in direct contact with timber – the wood may stain the fabric. Re-fold a stored quilt occasionally to avoid permanent crease marks. A few hours in the fresh air will get rid of any mustiness in a long-stored quilt, while a tumble drier on the cold air cycle will fluff up the batting.

Following page: An 'Attic Window' design by Susan McIver with a simple quilted pattern around the border.

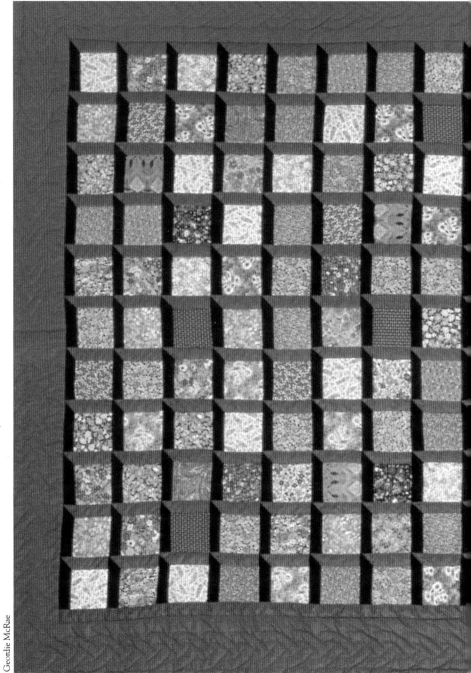

Geordie McRae

BEGINNER'S PROJECT

A DECORATIVE, quilted cushion makes an ideal first project. It is not large enough to be daunting to a beginner and yet it will provide you with enough quilting experience to give you confidence to tackle a more ambitious project the next time around.

Because of its size, the cushion top can be quilted without a frame; however I recommend that you use a frame or hoop to give you experience in handling one. In making this cushion top, I have used cotton lace as a trimming. There are also directions for making a self-ruffle, that is, a ruffle made in the same material as the cushion cover.

Materials for the cushion cover, ruffle and back you will need:
- 20   inches of white or off-white cotton fabric (or 1 5/8 yds if making a self-ruffle).
- 17   inch square of quilt batting.
- 17   inch square of old sheet or pillow case for backing when quilting the cushion top.
- 2 3/4   yds of lace, 3-4 1/2 inches in width.
- 1   cushion pad to fit a 16 inch square cushion.

To reproduce the design from this book, you will also need a pen and a large piece of graph paper.

Wash the cotton fabrics in warm water and detergent to remove any stiffener. Dry and iron fabric. Cut a 16 inch square from the material, fold this square into four and lightly iron in the creases. This will be the cushion top. The cushion design has been marked with a grid. Each square in this grid represents a 1 1/2 inch square on standard graph paper. Transfer the design onto a 15 3/4 inch sheet of graph paper, as shown in Fig. 19. Place the graph paper under the fabric square, find the center of the square, place this over the dot in the center of the design and trace the design onto the fabric. Remove the graph paper and iron out the creases. Make a quilt sandwich with this, the batting, and the old backing fabric. Pin and baste the three layers together and quilt as shown in 'Quilt Design'. Trim excess batting and backing material from the cushion top.

Making a lace ruffle:
Baste the raw edge of the lace either by machine or by hand, gathering as you go. Baste the lace to the top of the cushion cover, starting from the middle of one side, giving extra fullness to the corners.

Machine sew the lace in place with a 1/4 inch seam allowance.

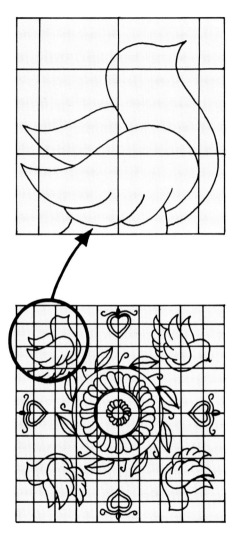

Fig. 19. Transferring the design to graph paper.

Making a self ruffle:

Cut four strips from the cotton fabric, each measuring 7 x 33 inches.

Sew strips right side together to form a circle of fabric. Fold and iron the strip in half lengthways, wrong sides together. The folded edge is the finished, or outside edge of the ruffle. Baste the ruffle around the seam edge, gathering as you go. Pin or baste the ruffle to the cushion top, making extra gathers around the corners so the ruffle will puff out. Sew the ruffle in with a 1/4 inch allowance and blindstitch the join between the two ruffle edges.

Making the cushion back:

Cut two pieces of fabric each measuring 16 x 10 1/2 inches .

Fold one of the long sides of each piece of fabric over twice, making a 1/2 inch hem, and machine sew in place. Pin the lace or cotton ruffle to the cushion top. Place one of the cushion back pieces over the cushion top, right sides together. Machine sew along three sides, just inside the machine line for the ruffle seam. Repeat with the other piece of cushion back. Fold both pieces over to the back of the cushion and fit the cushion pad inside the cover.

*A crazy patch jacket and hexagonal quilt, both designed by Judith Burgess,
in a country garden setting.*

INDEX